Pretty Is Me

THE PINK GLITTERY SKIRT AND WHITE POLKA-DOT TIGHTS

Written by Jada Lewis

Copyright © 2022 by Jada Lewis

Pretty is ME
Authored by Jada Lewis

All rights reserved. No part of this book may be used or reproduced in any manner whatsoever without written permission.

Illustrations by Iqra Zahid

I would like to dedicate this book to three special teachers who saw the gift of writing in me when I didn't recognize it myself. Those phenomenal women are: Mrs. Henderson, Ms. McKelvey, and Mrs. Chandler. I thank you all for challenging me during my time as a student, because those challenges ultimately led me to become an author! I love you all dearly.

The day had finally come for Draiyah to start her first week of kindergarten.

She wasn't thinking about meeting her new teacher, making new friends, or doing much of anything new.

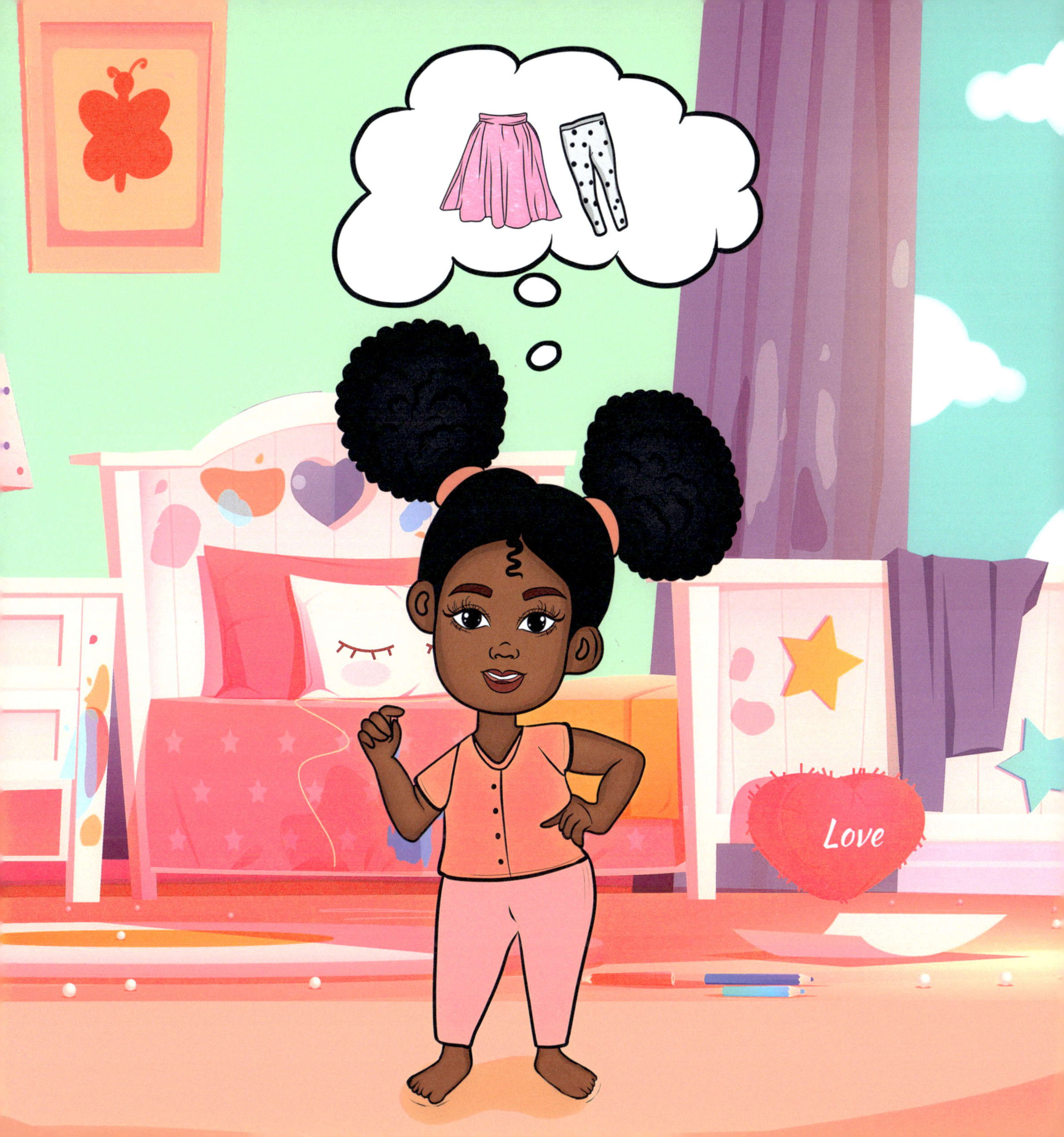
Love

Draiyah was just excited to wear her pink, glittery skirt and white polka-dot tights.

"*Wake up,*" her mom yelled through the door. "It's time to get dressed for your first day of school!"

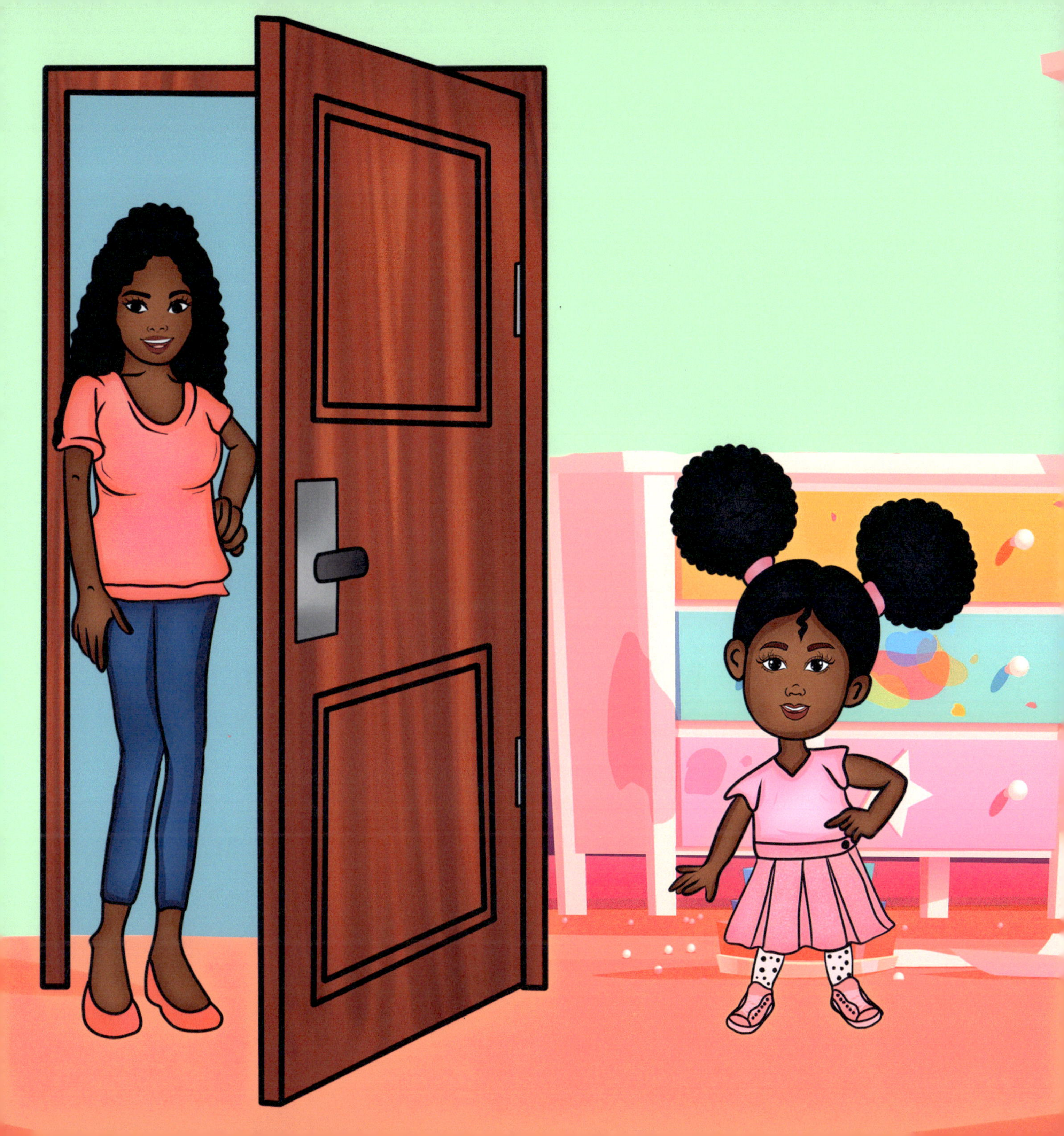

Little did she know, Draiyah had already been awake.

In fact, she was standing in the mirror blushing at her outfit.

"My day is going to be great," she said to herself proudly. "Thank you, special skirt and special tights for making me pretty."

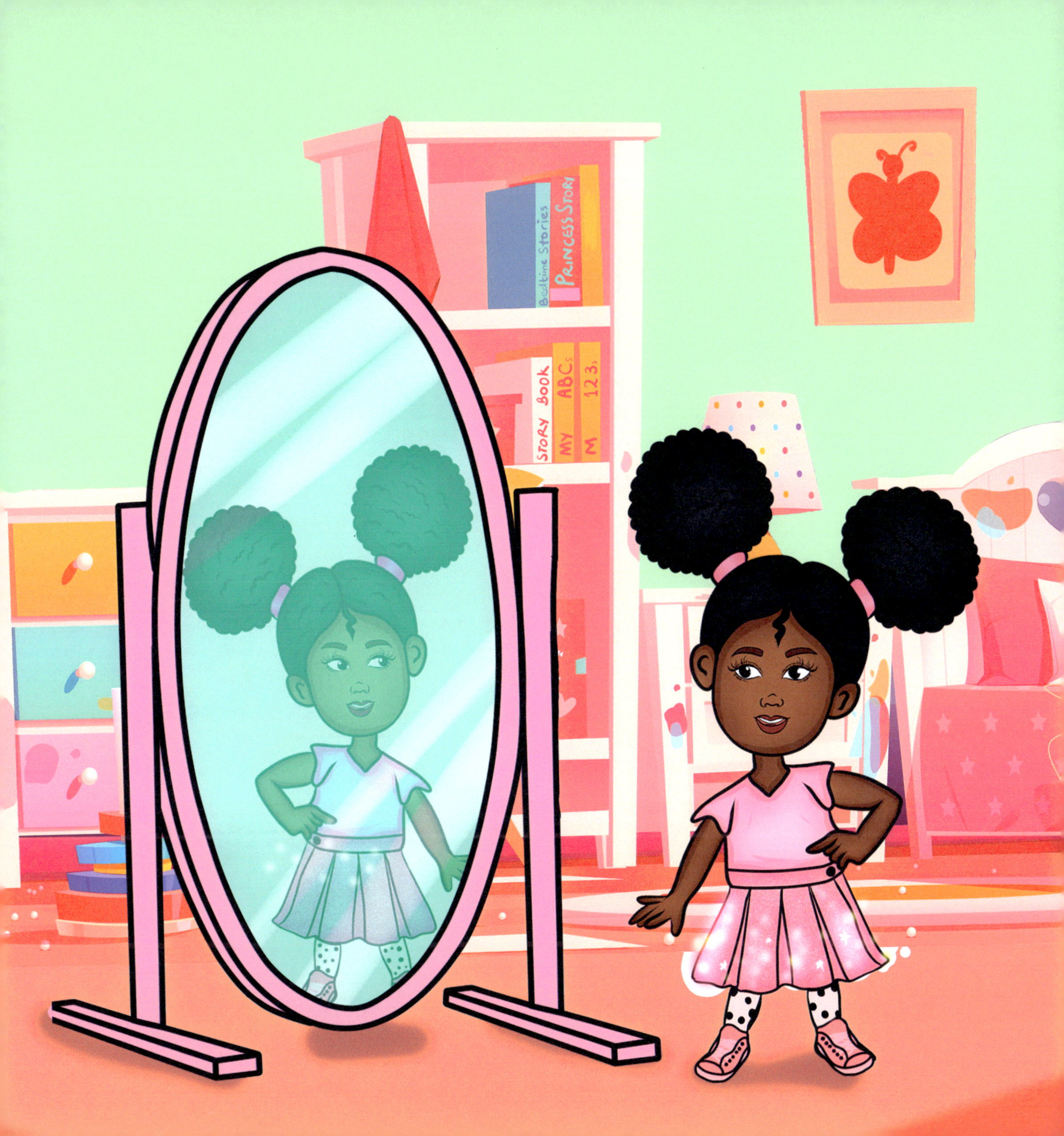
Bedtime Stories
PRINCESS STORY
STORY BOOK
MY ABCs

As Draiyah walked into class, her teacher was greeting everyone with a warm welcome.

"*Hello my young stars,*" Ms. Hannigan exclaimed. "*Let's start with introductions!*"

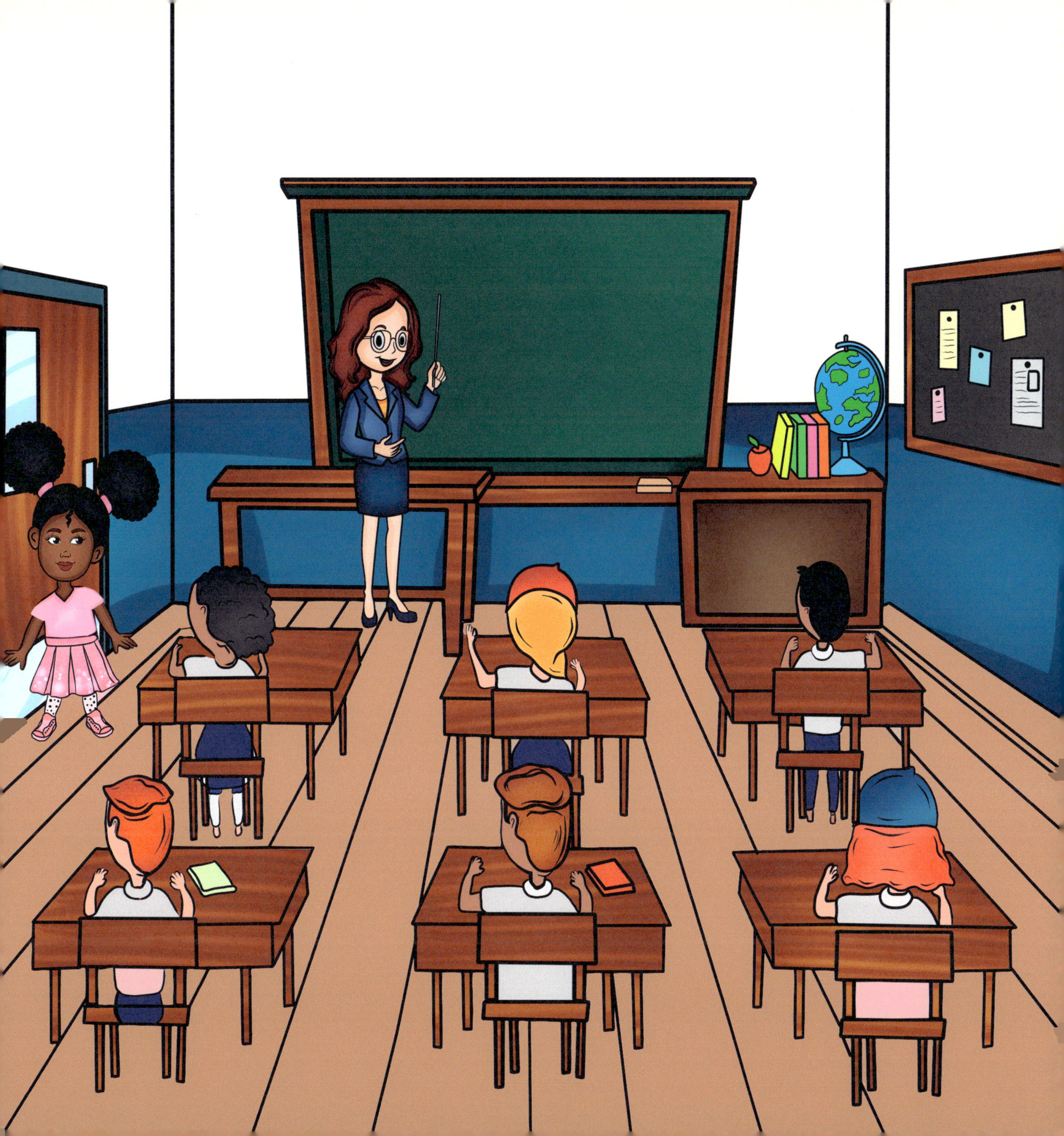

When it was Draiyah's turn to introduce herself, she became very shy.

She had no idea why all the other kids were staring at her, but they were actually amazed at her pink, glittery skirt and white polka-dot tights.

"Hi, my name is Draiyah," she said. "My favorite color is pink."

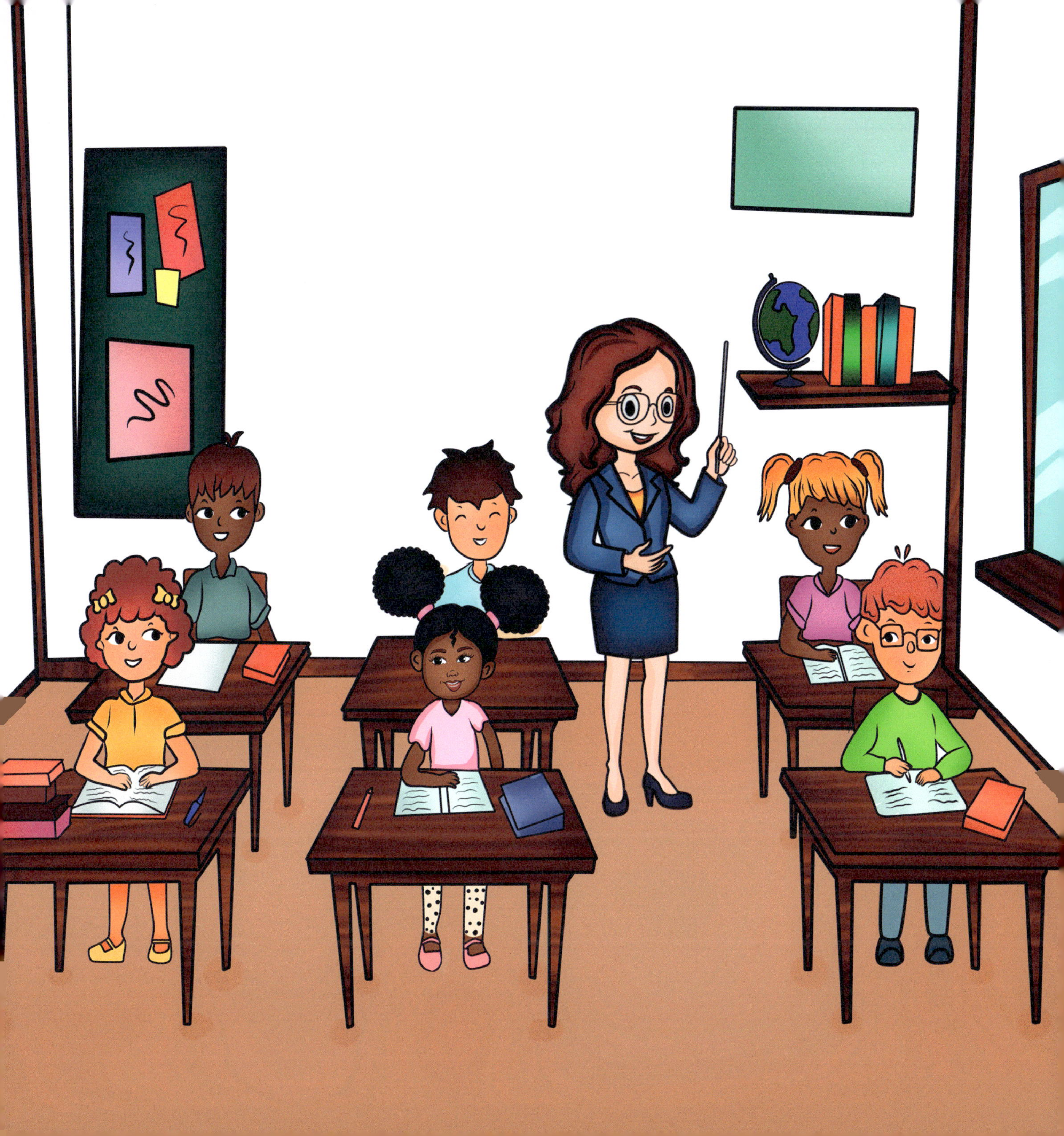

She sat back down in her seat to a tap on the shoulder.

"I like your skirt and your polka-dot tights," her classmate whispered.

"Your pink glittery skirt and polka-dot tights are really pretty," said another.

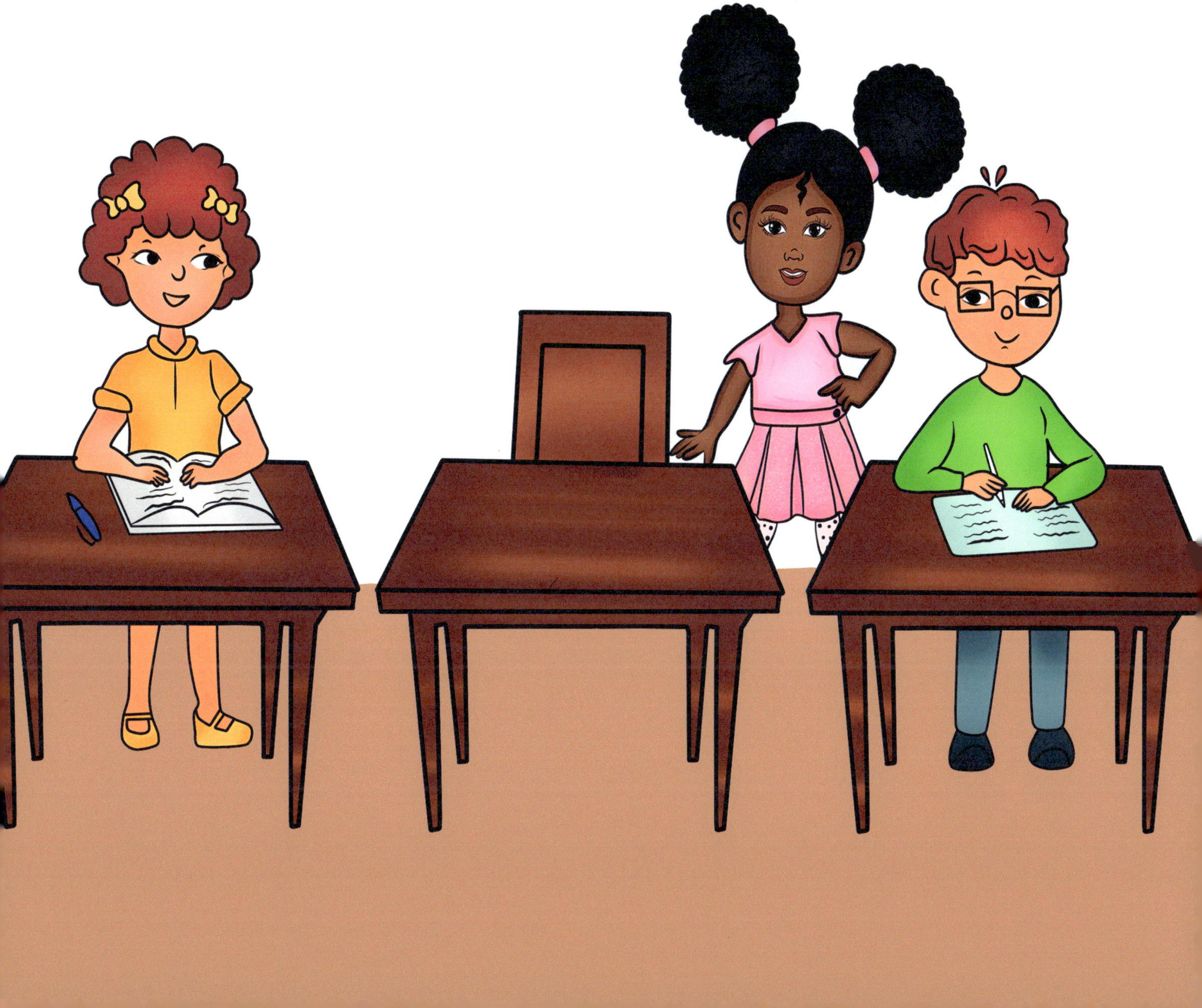

After school, all Draiyah could think about was how pretty she felt.

"Mommy, I had the best day ever," she bragged. "My classmates really liked my pink, glittery skirt and white polka-dot tights."

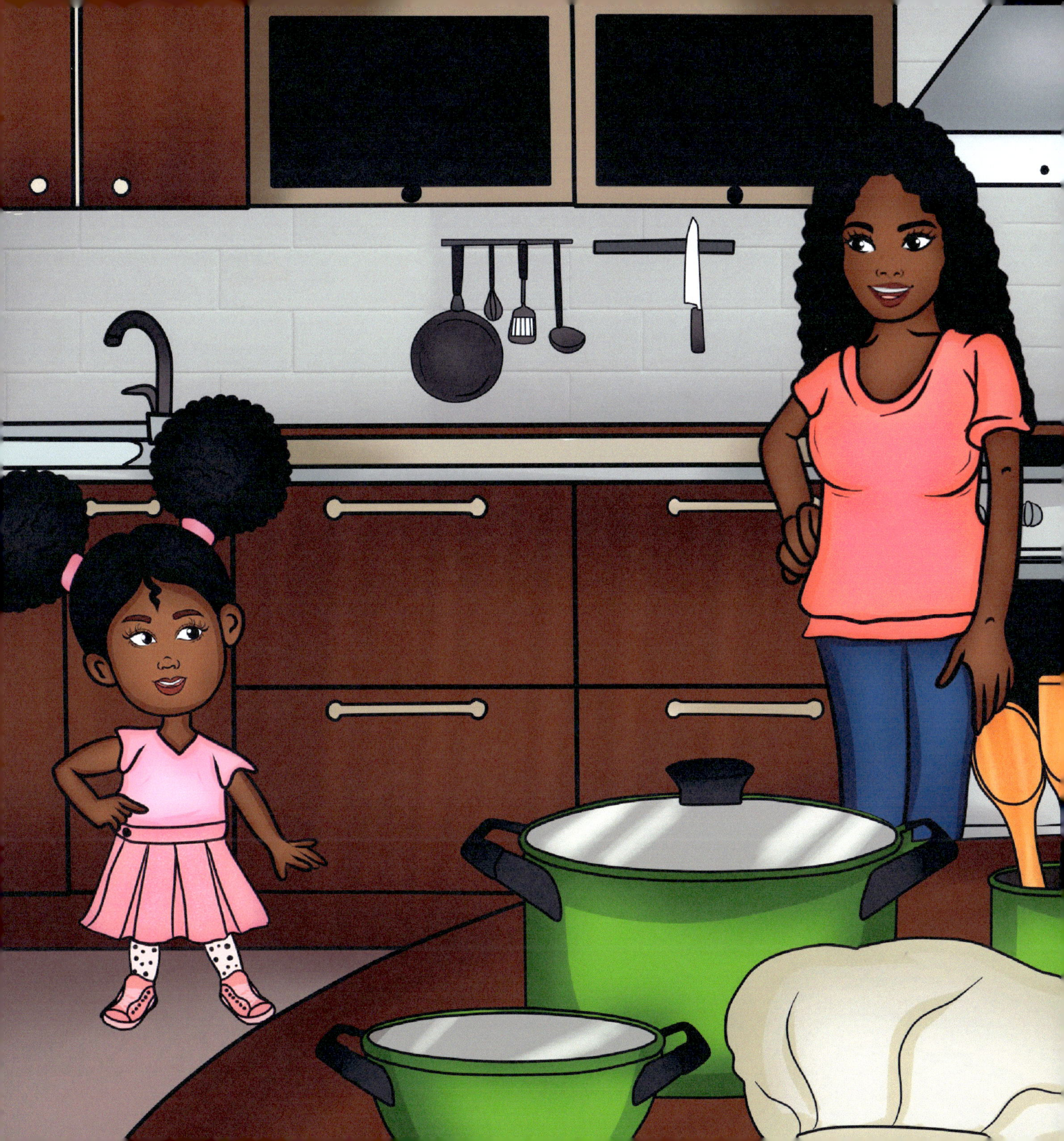

"Well, you know you have to wear something different tomorrow," her mom said.

"No I don't," insisted Draiyah. "I can just wear my skirt and my tights again."

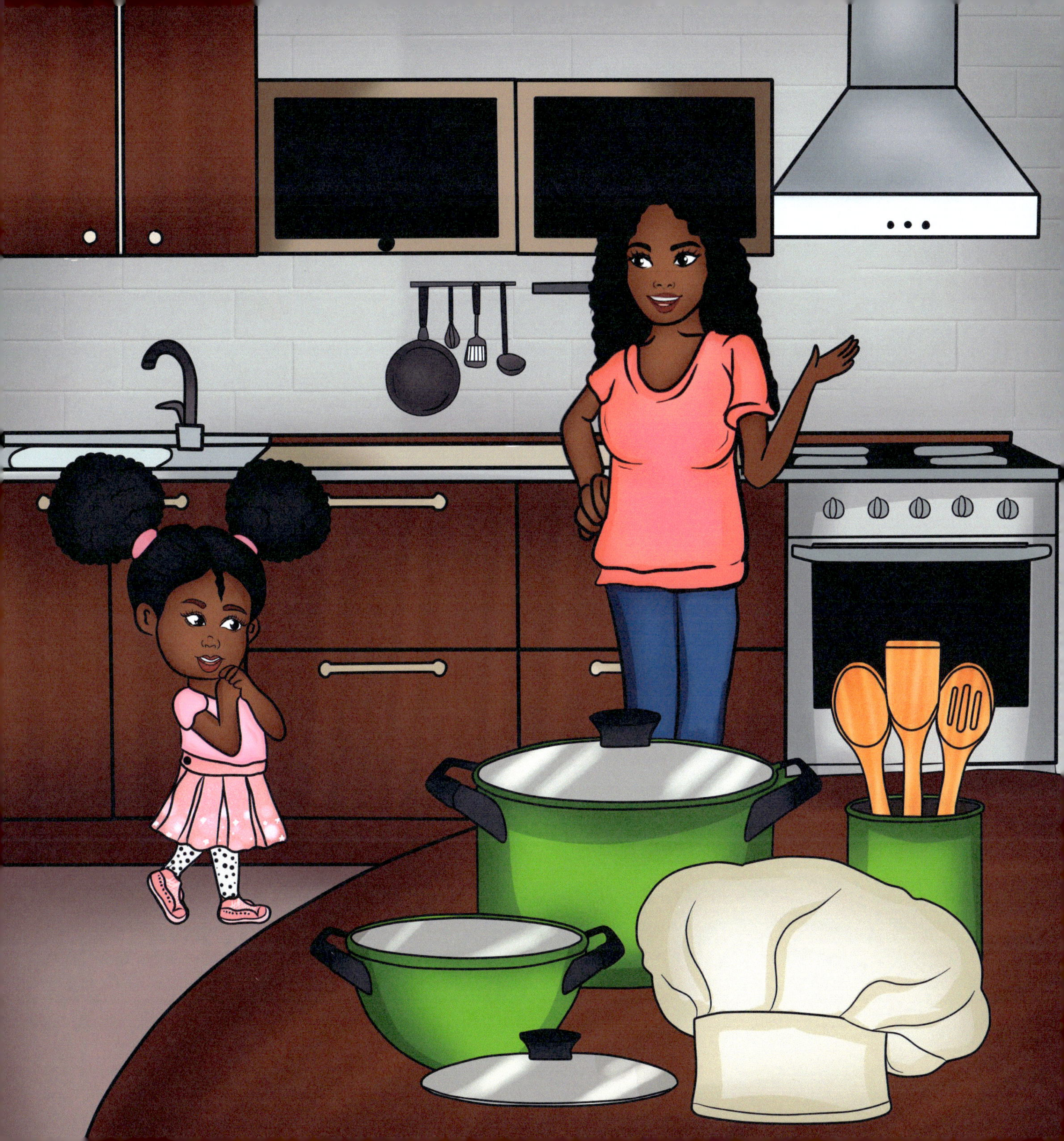

Her mom turned down the idea;
Instead, Draiyah had to wear
blue jeans to school.

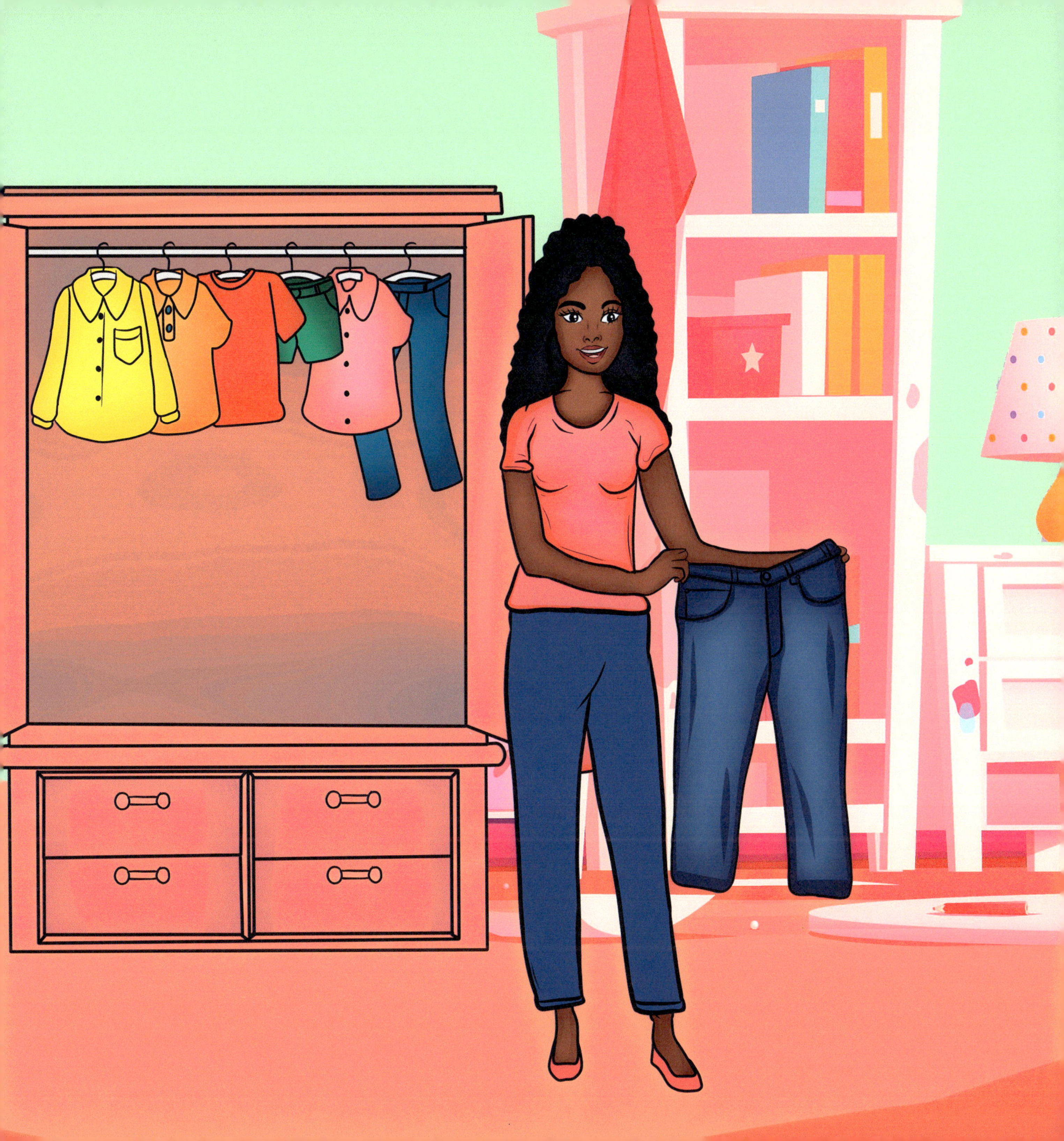

So, for the rest of the night, she decided to pout.

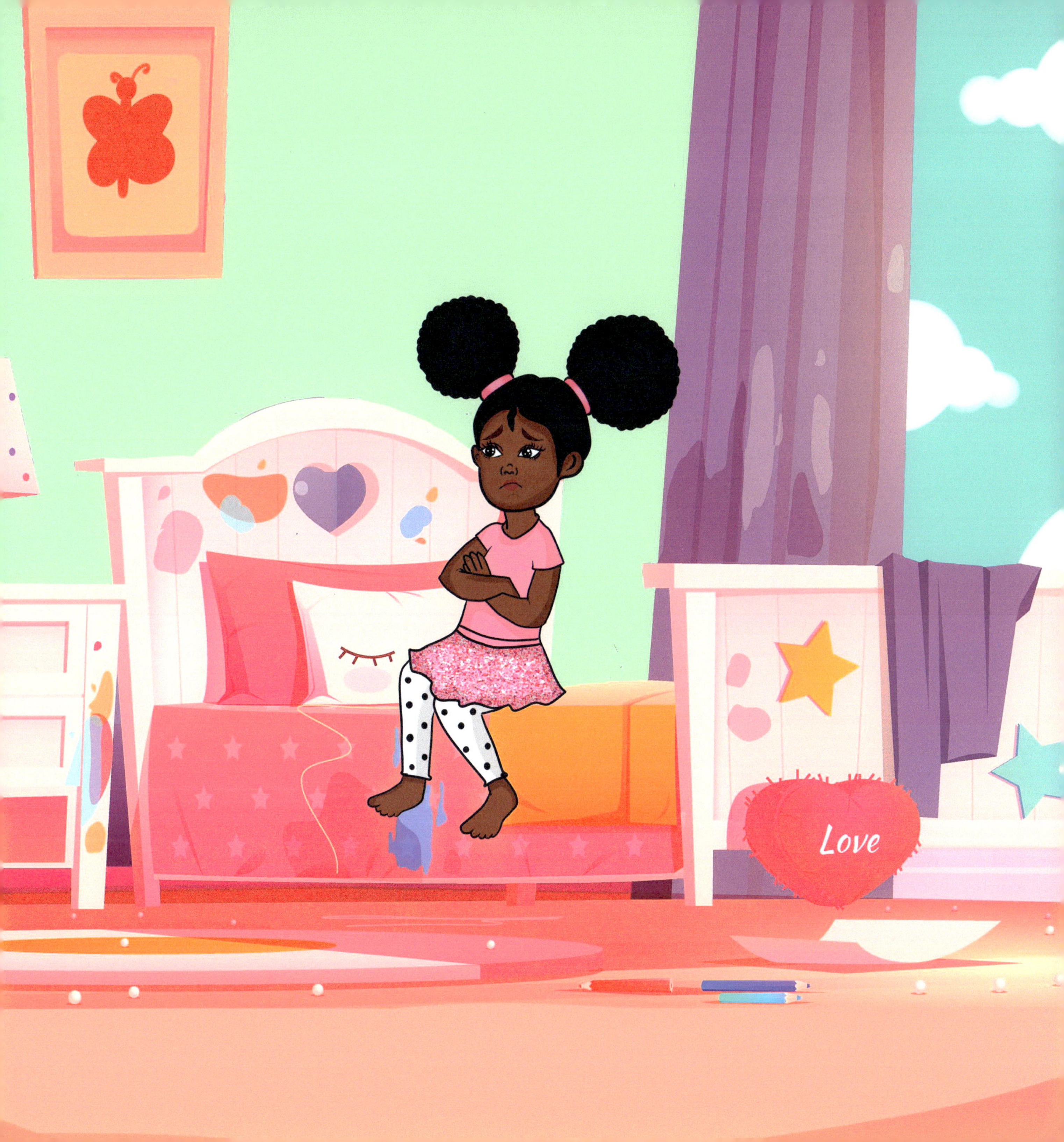
Love

She pouted at dinner.

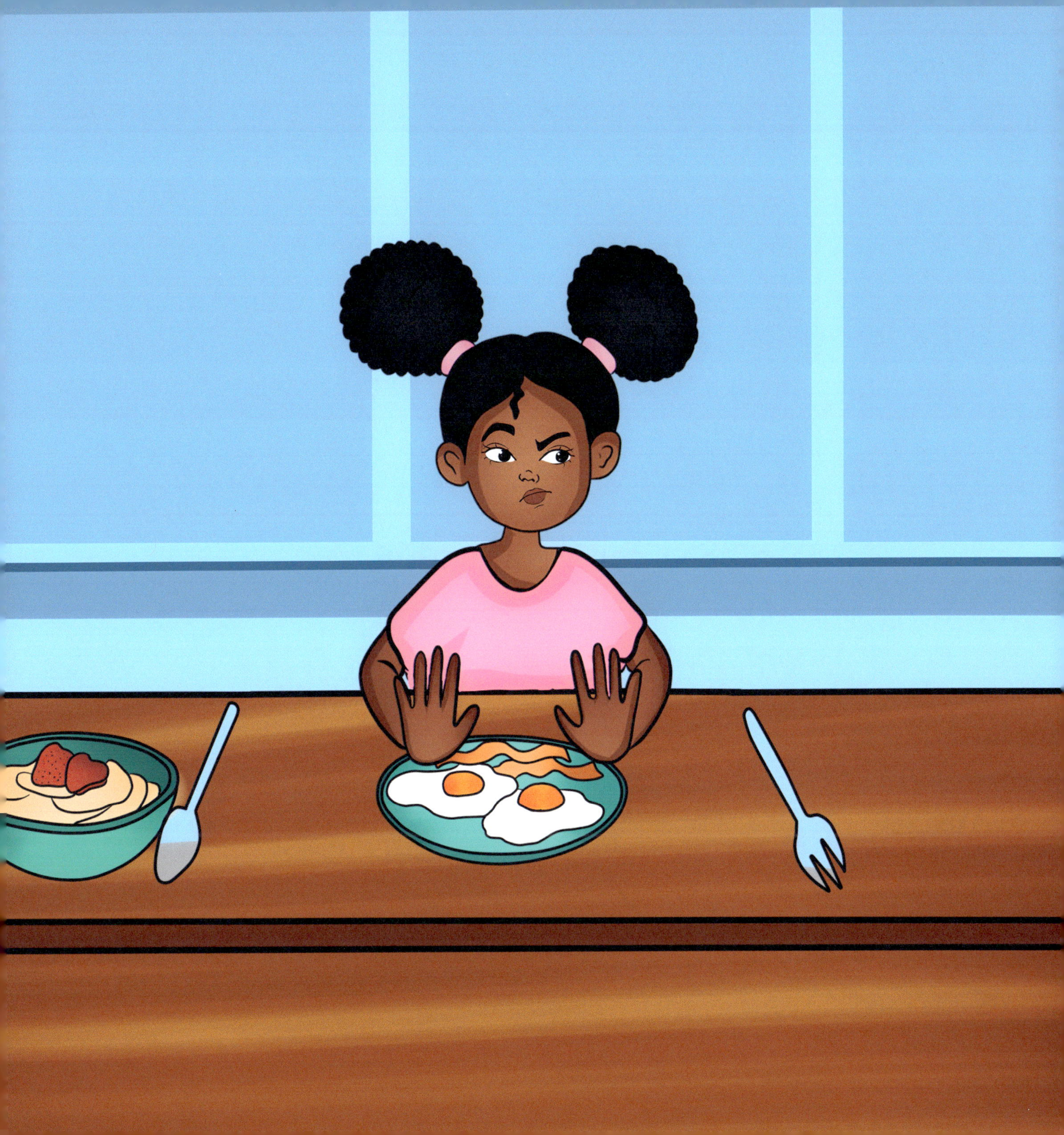

She pouted at bath time.

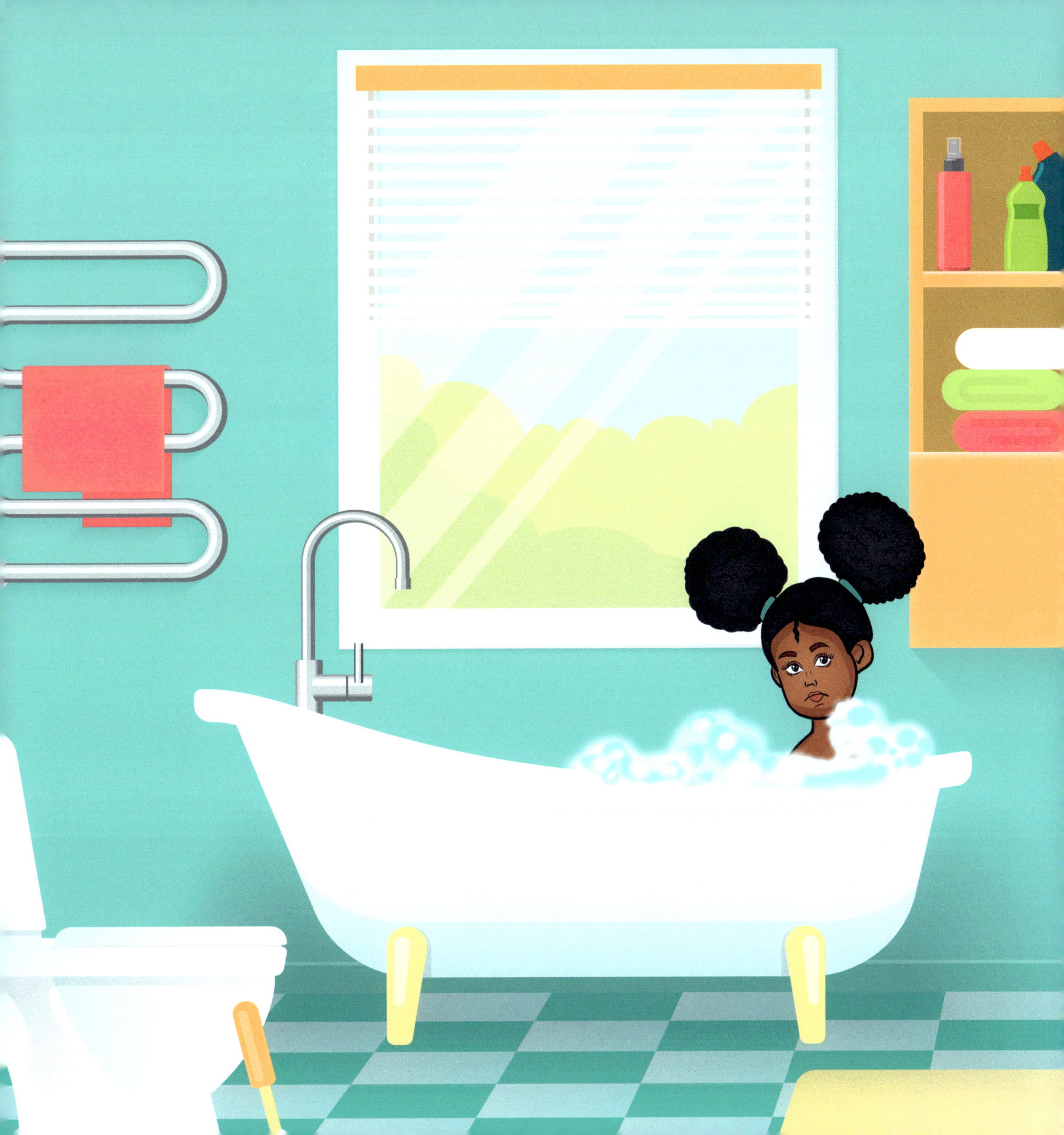

She even pouted in her sleep.

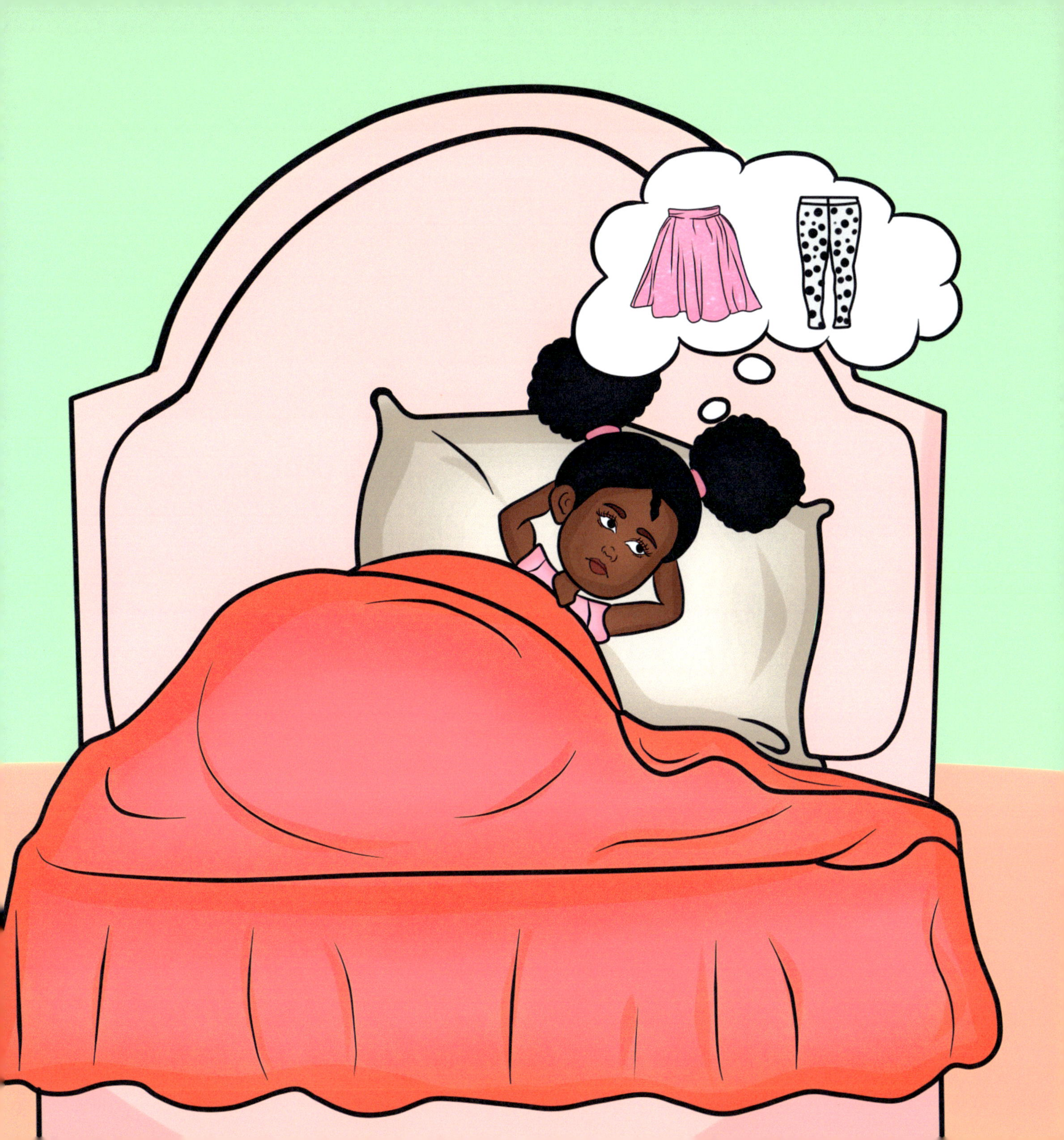

When morning came, Draiyah thought
of a master plan.

She knew she couldn't wear her skirt,
so she found a purple dress instead.

Love

Her mom was standing at the door with her arms folded in disbelief.

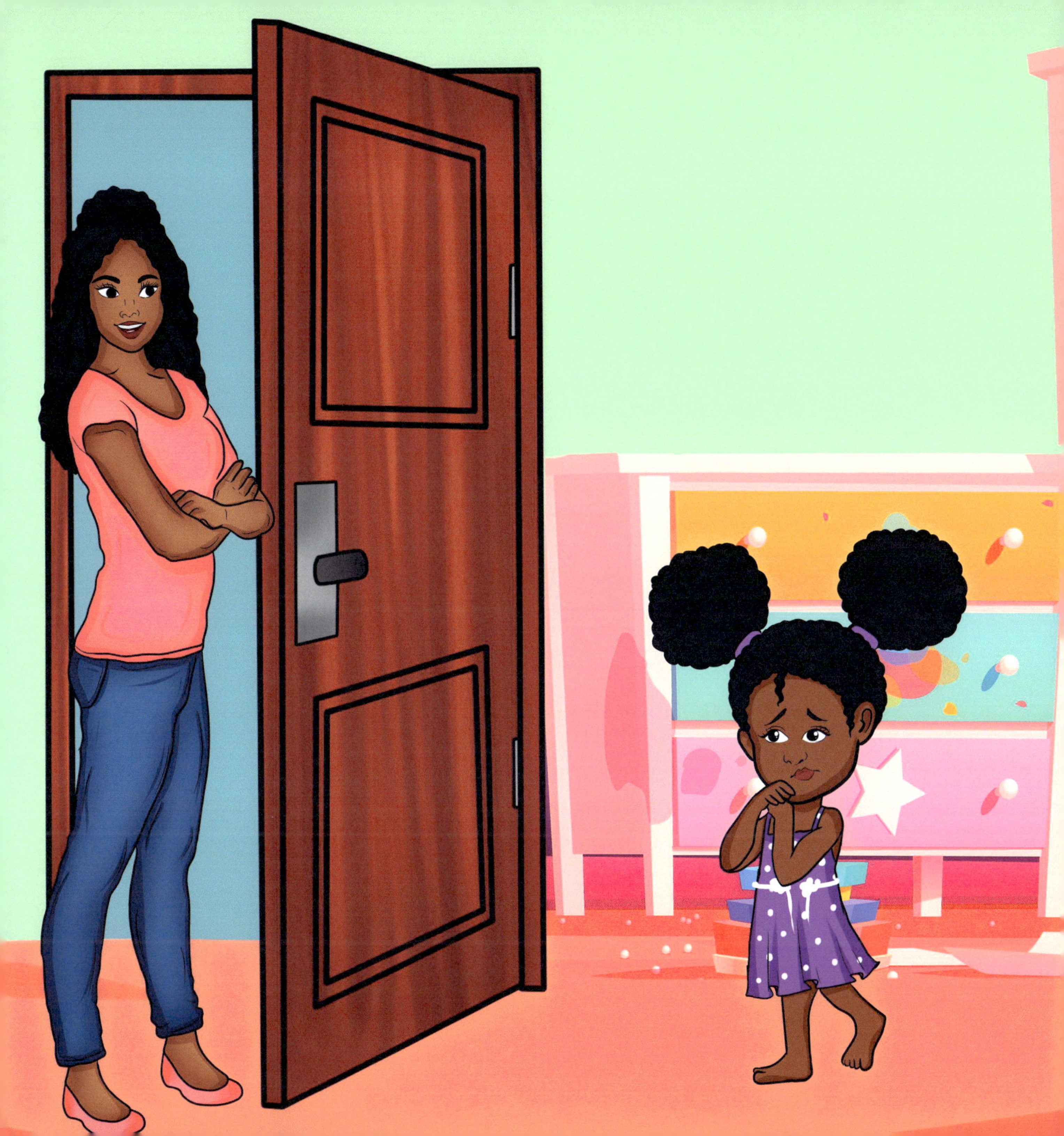

"You can't wear that dress. It's too cold outside, and you have no tights to wear underneath."

"But mommy please," begged Draiyah. *"I have to wear a dress or a skirt, or I won't be pretty today."*

Love

"That is nonsense," her mom explained. "Always remember—it is not the skirt or the tights that make you pretty, but the magic power is in you."

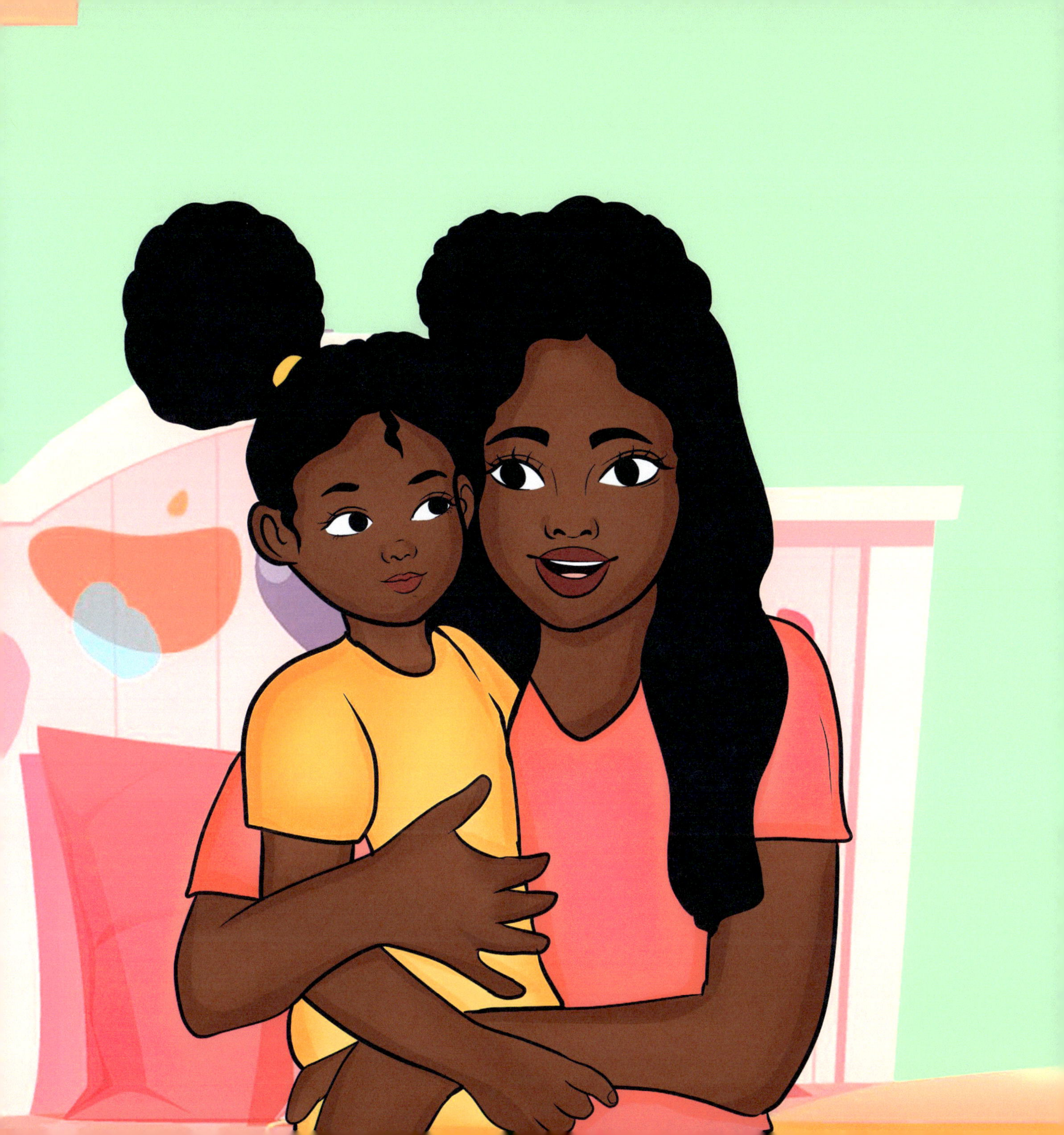

Draiyah didn't quite understand exactly what her mom meant, so she blurted out the questions floating in her head.

"What do you mean?!"

"Are you saying I have magic?!"

"Do I really have powers?!"

"You have GOT to be kidding me, right?!"

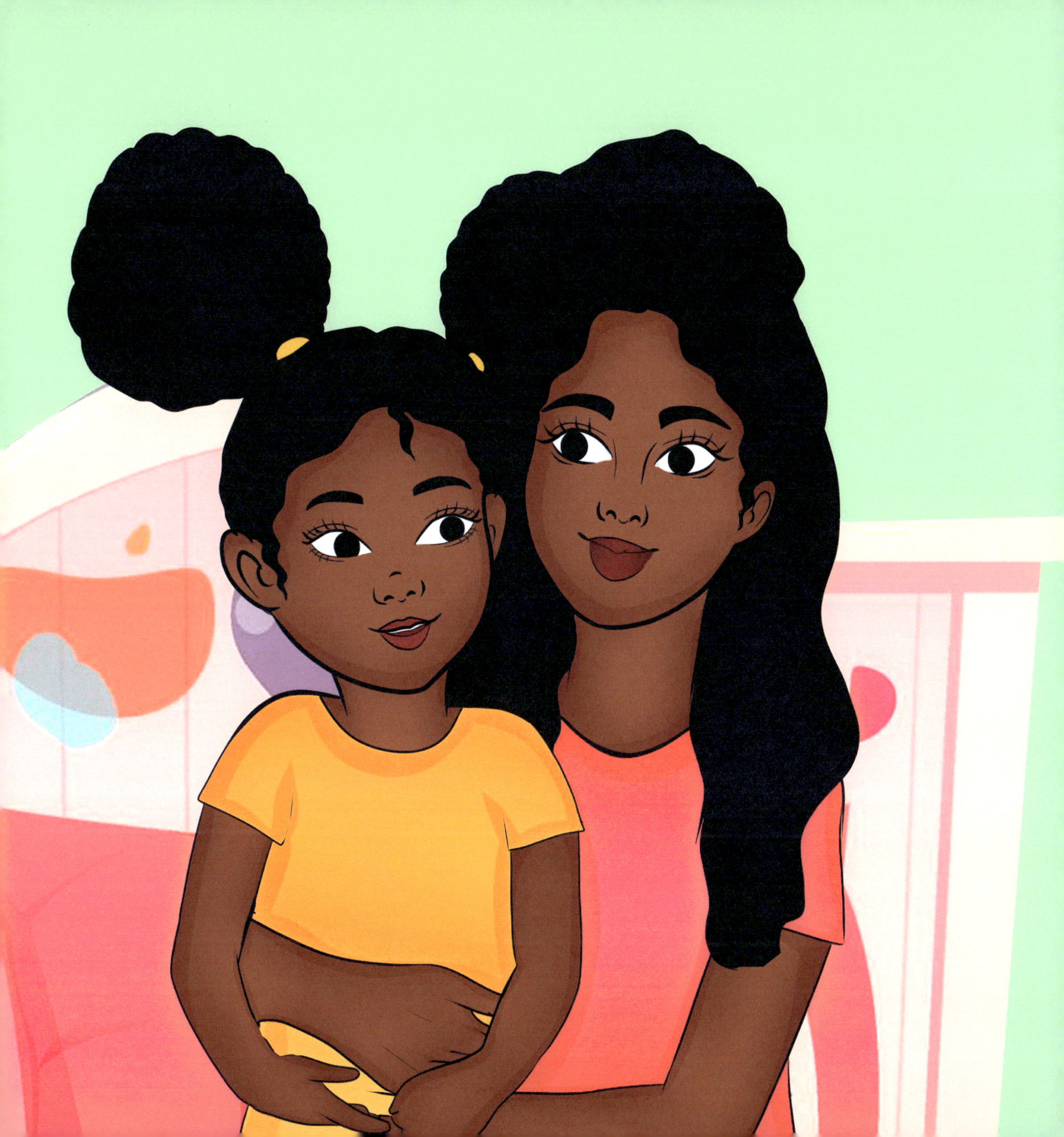

When she arrived at school, Draiyah sat in her seat and looked around to see if anyone would notice.

There were no taps on the shoulder or praises from her classmates.

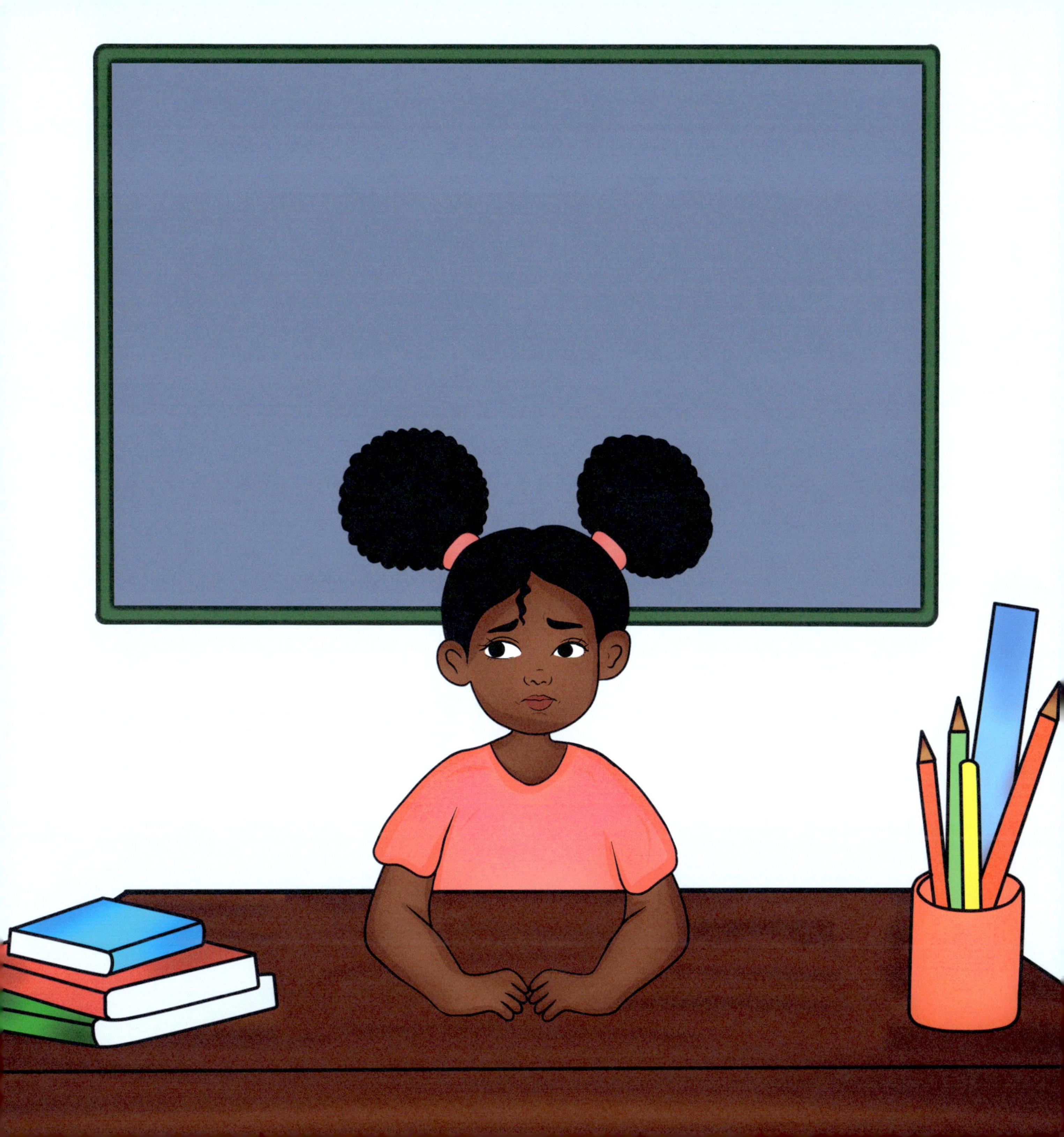

"So much for my secret powers," she mumbled sadly.

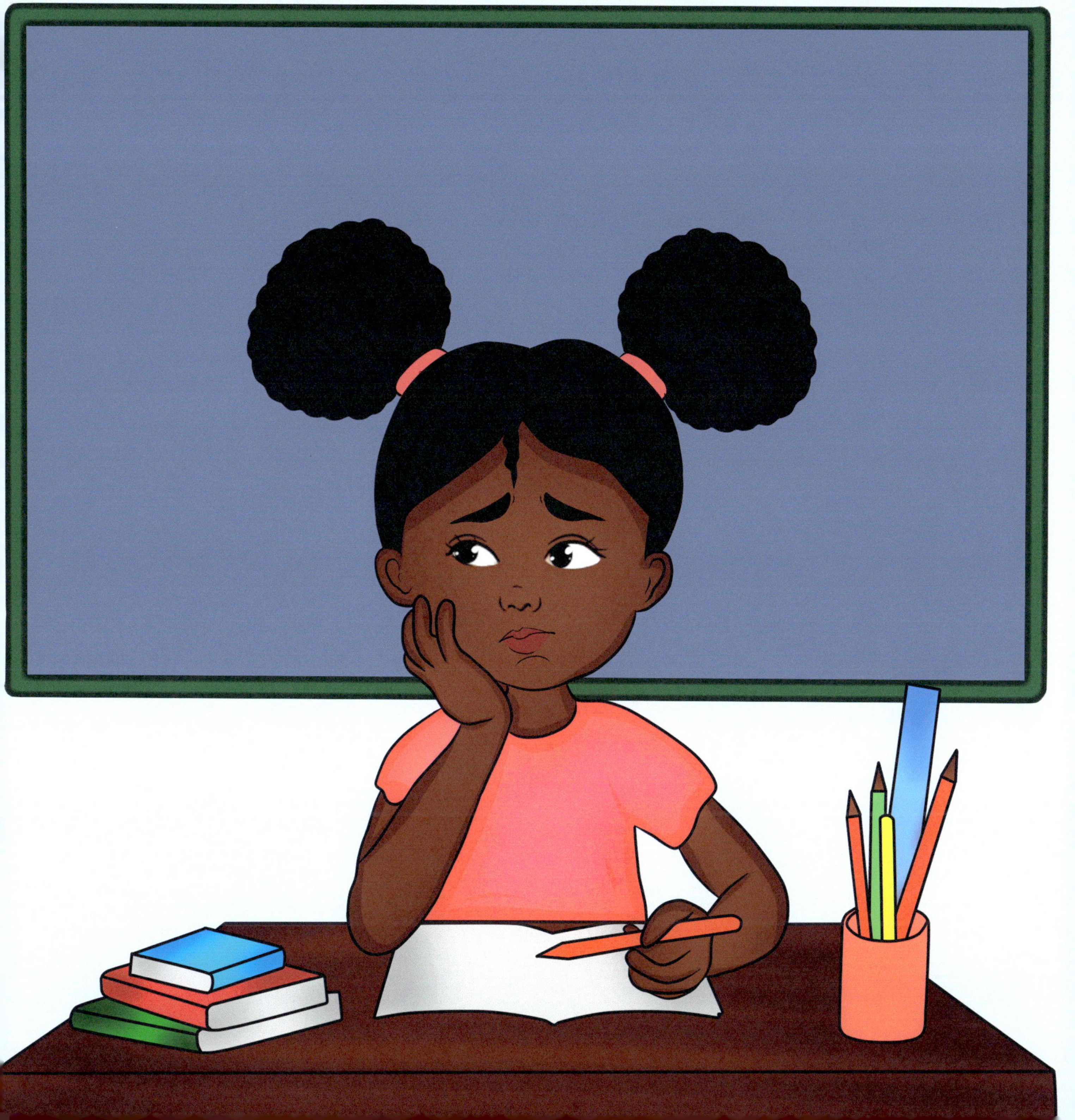

At recess, Draiyah decided to play alone on the swing set.

She didn't want to be bothered, and she didn't feel very pretty either.

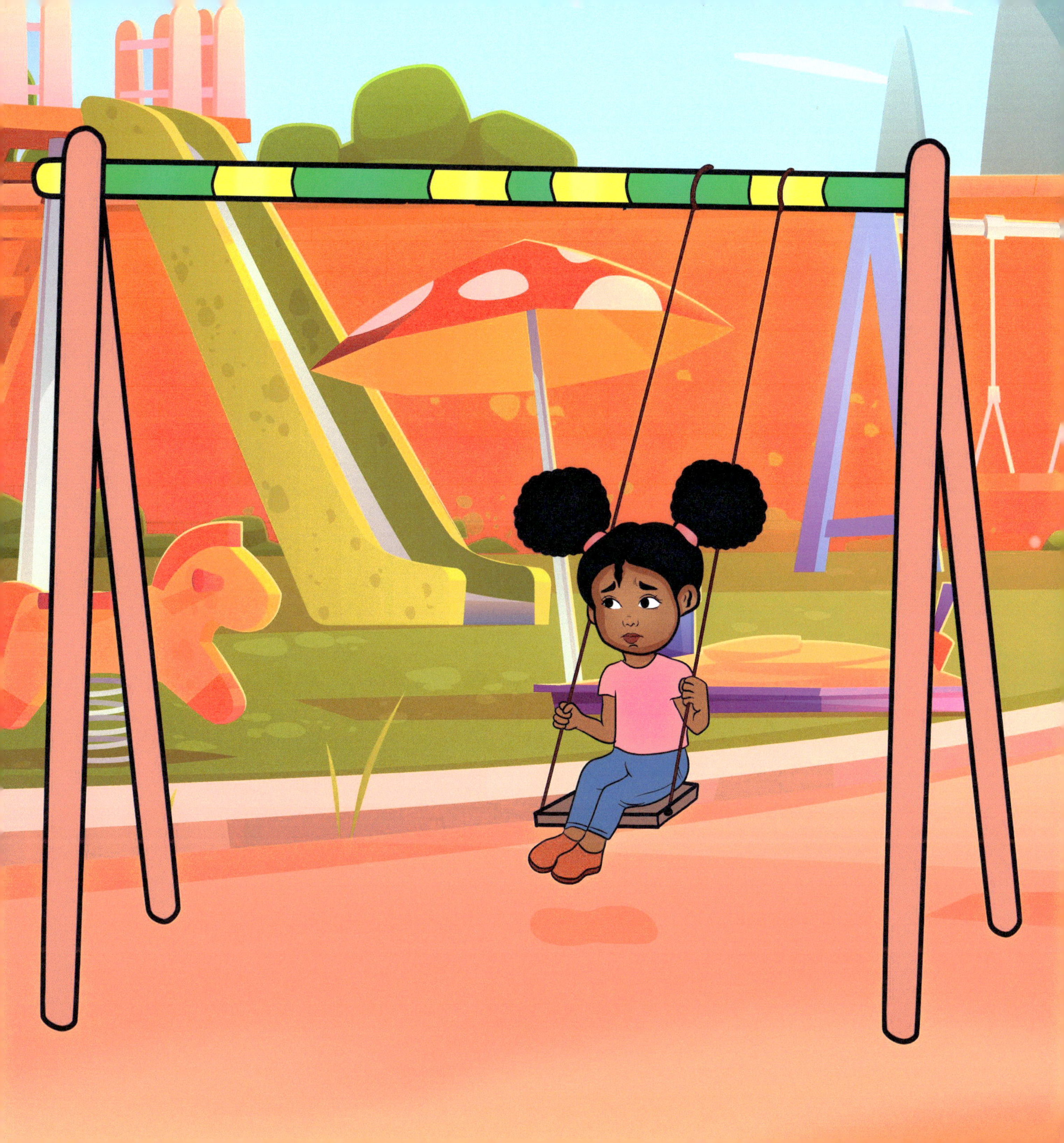

Two girls from her class stomped over in their glittery skirts and polka-dot tights with their nostrils flared.

"*What are you wearing?!*" one yelled.

"*Yeah! Blue jeans aren't pretty,*" sassed the other.

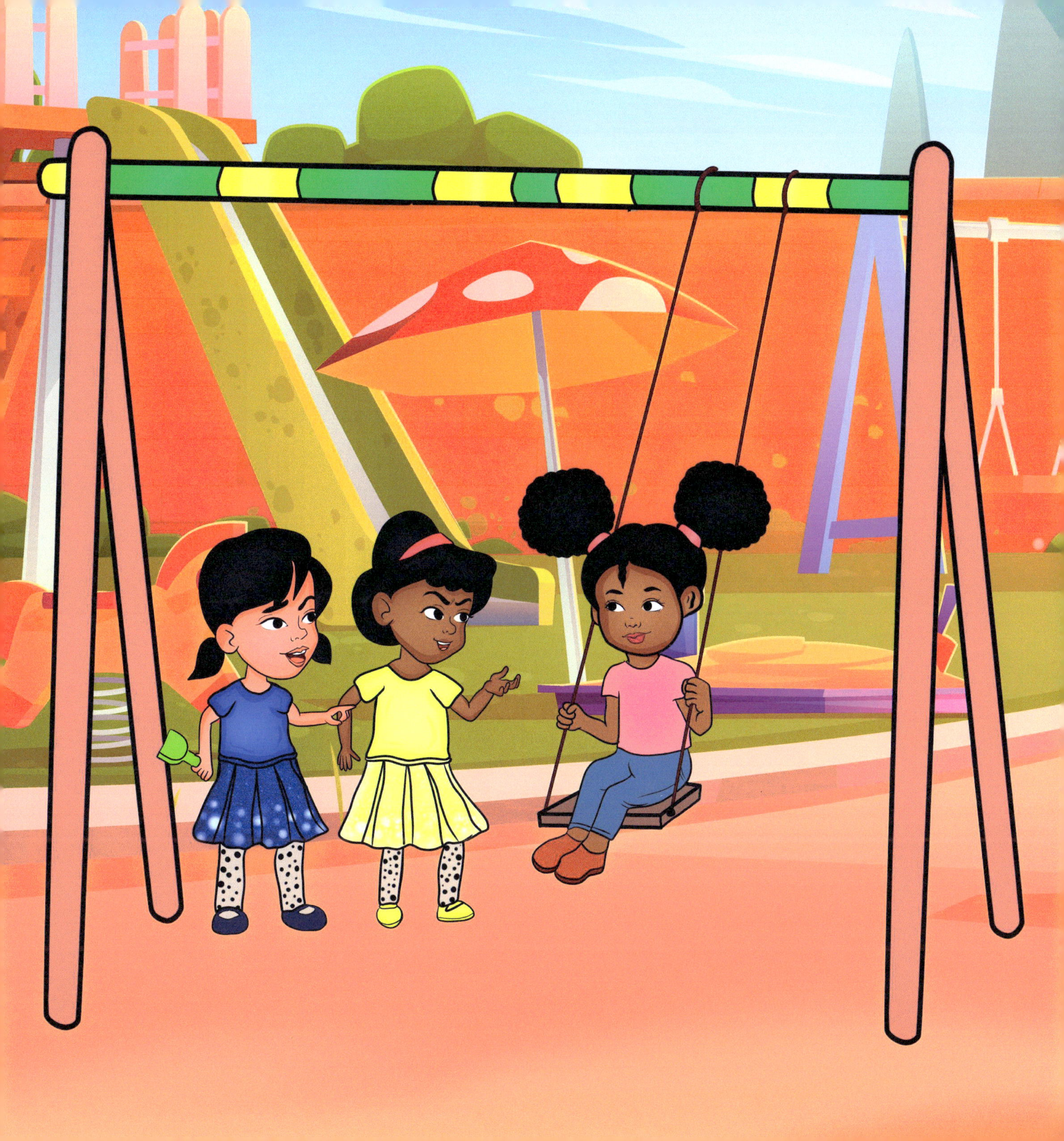

Draiyah wanted to run away and bawl up under a tree, but she remembered two important words from the talk she had with her mother— 'magic' and 'power.'

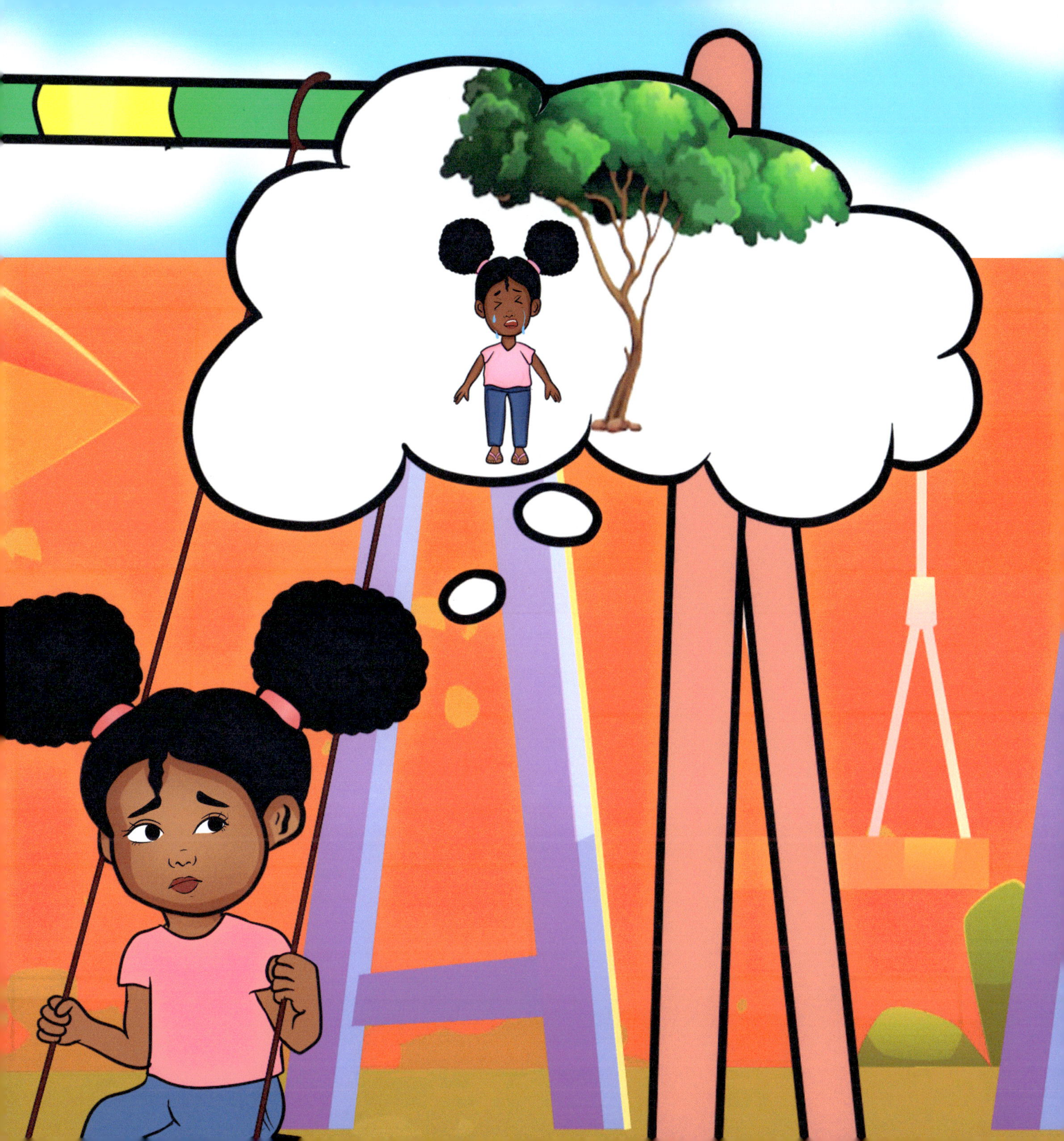

"We have a magic power to make our clothes pretty," Draiyah stated bravely. "Pretty is inside of us—not in the clothes we wear."

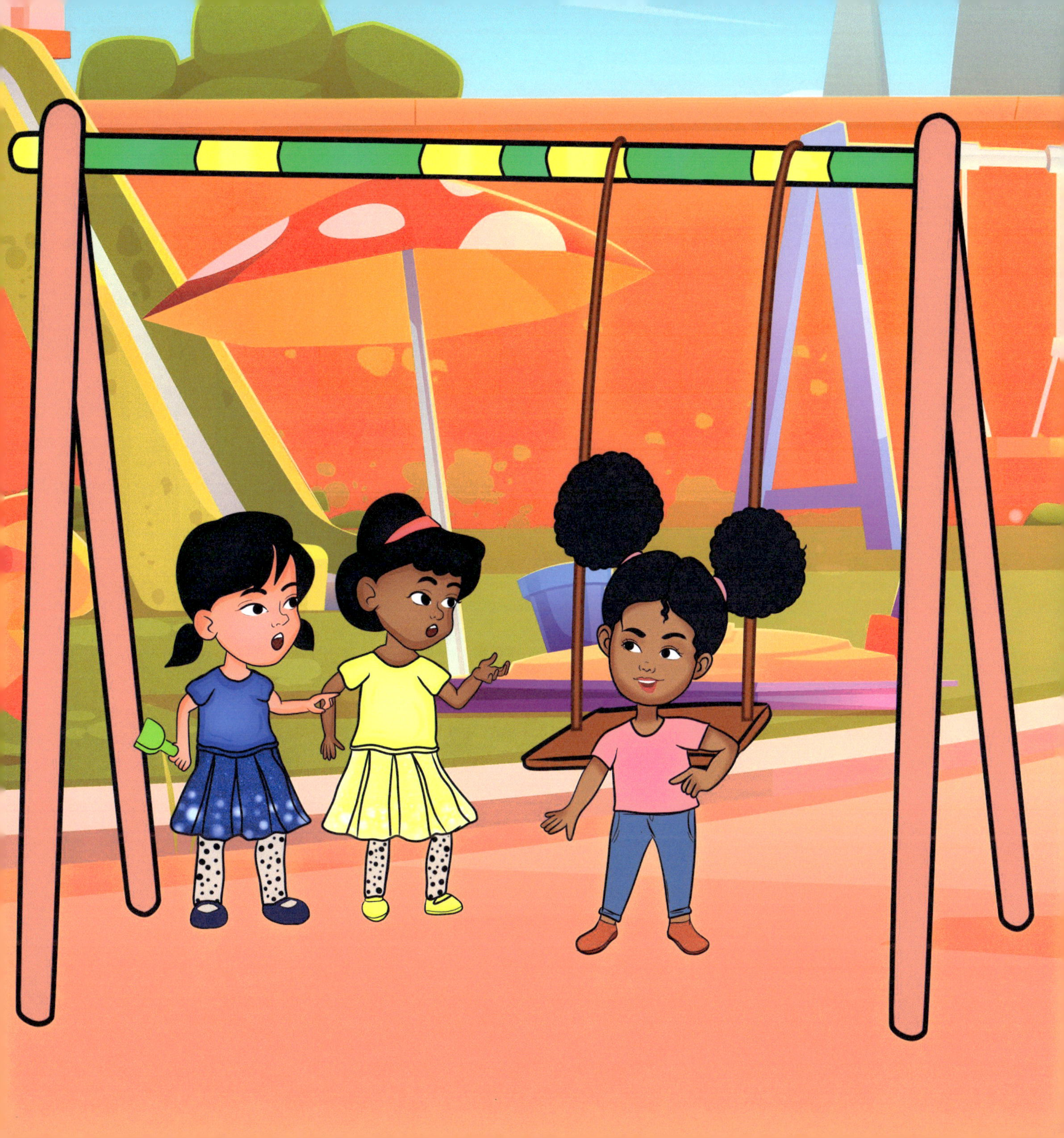

The two girls stood there in total shock.

"*MAGIC?!*" one said excitedly.

"That is so awesome!" shouted the other.

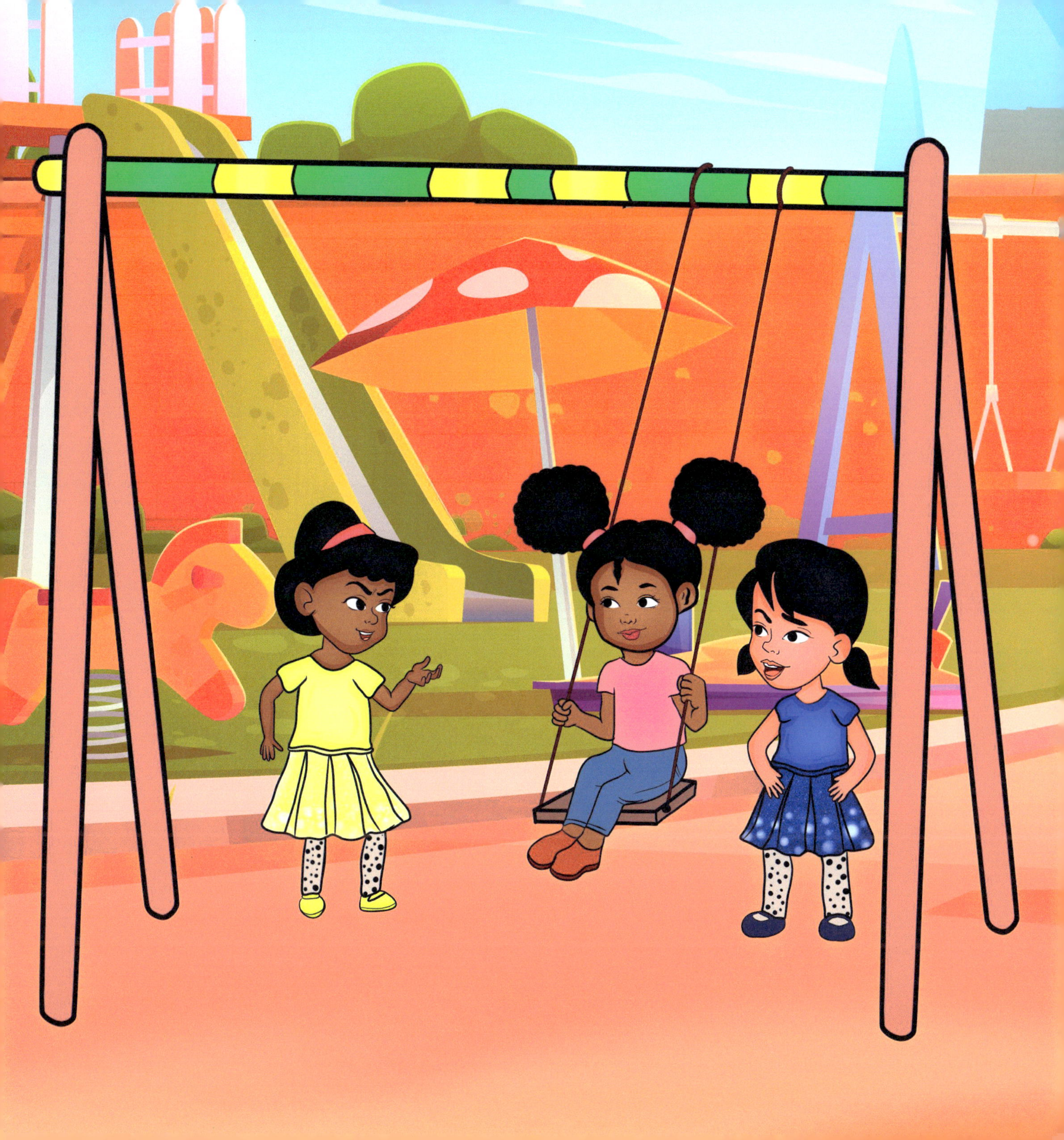

Draiyah and her new friends ran off into the grass and chased each other with joy.

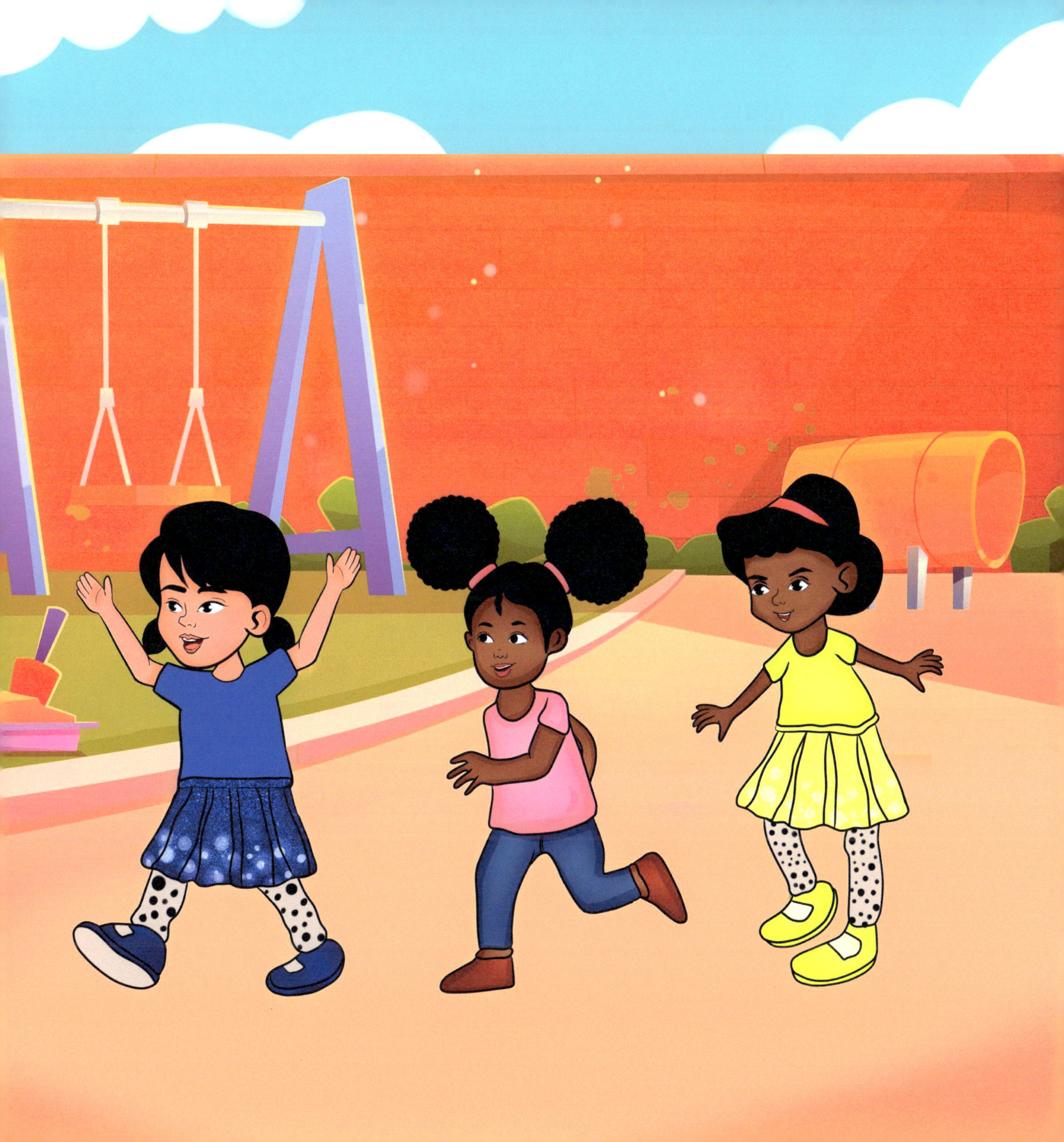

After school she couldn't wait to tell her mom how her day went.

"Mommy I had the best day ever," Draiyah gushed. "Even though I didn't get to wear my pink, glittery skirt and white polka-dot tights—I still felt pretty."

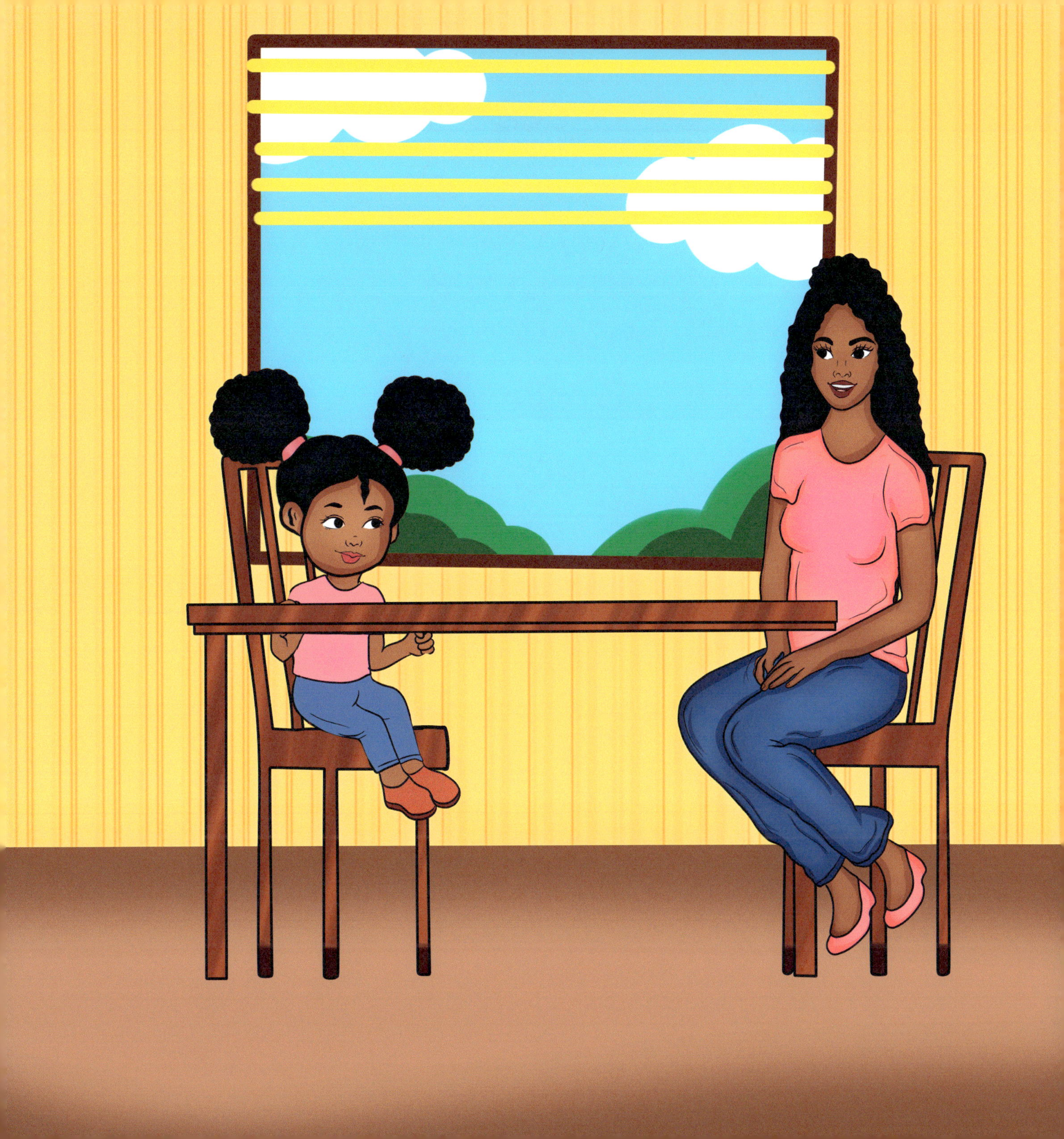

Made in the USA
Columbia, SC
08 November 2024